ANGELS ASSIGNED TO YOU

MICHELLE CORRAL

Published by

LifeBridge
Books
P.O. BOX 49428
CHARLOTTE, NC 28277

Printed in the United States of America.

DEDICATION

This book is lovingly dedicated to my beloved lifelong companion and spouse, Manuel Corral, and to our two children, Rose and Joel, the loves of our lives.

I would also like to dedicate this book to the courage and inspiration given to all by our Down syndrome friends.

SPECIAL THANKS

To my dearest sister in Christ, Katy Bennett, who faithfully transcribed my notes and sermons. Also to Matt and Tanya Schweiger for their hours of help.

$\mathcal{F}$OREWORD

$\mathcal{I}$t was in the early 1990's that I had the privilege of meeting and getting to know my very good friend, Dr. Michelle Corral. She is a General in the body of Christ, who walks in character and integrity. Most of her time is spent studying the Bible with her Lord, or in adoration—in the solitude of that place deep within her interior castle, communing and praying to the "Lover of Her Soul."

In this book, *Angels Assigned to You,* Michelle shows you how the Word of God is full of angelic activities in the heavenlies, as well as on the earth. She emphasizes that if we ignore the existence of the angelic realm we would literally deny the providence, provision, and protection which has been provided for everyone. This divine protection is especially for the children of God who choose to walk according to His covenant, through prayer, intercession, faith, fasting, and thus commissioning and asking the Lord to release the angelic hosts that are available and are on assignment to us.

As with Daniel in the Bible, angels were released to do battle on his and heaven's behalf, against principalities, powers, rulers of darkness in high places, or even pulling down strongholds. Angels are at work on our behalf not only as individuals but for our family members and loved ones. In Daniel's case, angels were sent to pull down strongholds in a nation, to gain territory for the Kingdom of God.

In 1979, Michelle was traveling on one of her first mission trips with her mother, Joanne Petronella. They landed at JFK airport and took a New York subway to downtown Manhattan. In the hustle and bustle of arriving at the subway, they had too much luggage for two women to carry on their own. It was midnight! Out of nowhere a very muscular, young man came and helped them with their heavy luggage without even being asked—carrying it up the stairs to the street. That moment was one of Michelle's first encounters with an angel coming in the form of a man to help her carry out the work of God. In Hebrews 13:1, the Bible says, *"...for thereby some have entertained angels unawares."* The Lord had already prepared the angel ahead of time to take care of His servants. Once the assignment was completed, the angel vanished.

In Matthew 6:33, we are told to *"Seek ye first the*

*Kingdom of God, His righteousness; and all these
things shall be added unto you."* This is why we
should never pursue experiences but rather seek Jesus.
Don't forget there are also one-third of the angels that
fell with Lucifer (Satan) to the earth who are *not* holy
and good. For this reason angels are not to be
worshiped.

Through her intense study on this topic, Michelle
very capably explains the different types of angels in
Revelation 4:6 and Isaiah 6:2-3. The angels with six
wings called "the seraphim" are forever before the
throne of God in heaven continually singing, crying
and exalting "Holy, Holy, Holy." They say this because
of the infinite and continual revelations of His
splendor and holiness, which are always flowing from
within Him in the beauty of His holiness, through His
words and actions.

Even though angels are forever beholding His
majesty and beauty, they look with wonder at us, the
human race, knowing that because of the cross of
Calvary, we, who choose to accept Him, Jesus Christ,
as Lord and Savior, can know and walk in His
redemption, which was not made available to the
angels.

Because of God the Father's love for mankind, He sent His only begotten Son to pay the ultimate sacrifice and die for our sins, so we can and will live with Jesus eternally.

— *Suzanne Hinn*

CONTENTS

CHAPTER ONE

SECRET SERVICE FOR THE SAINTS

Bless the Lord, ye his angels, that
excel in strength, that do his commandments,
hearkening unto the voice of his word.

– PSALM 103:20

I am thrilled you are reading this book. Why? Because the study of angels is one of the most overlooked and misunderstood topics in Scripture.

Have you ever been captivated by the question, "Who are these invisible agents of God—and how do they affect my life?"

It is my prayer to attempt to solve some of the secret perplexities you have always hidden in your heart concerning angels.

On these pages you will encounter:

11

- How the ministries of angels are assigned on earth.
- How—in their secret service—they are servants to the saints.
- How their ministry to you has been bought and paid for through the blood of Jesus.

As we ponder this provocative subject, we will be careful to confine all the mysteries that mobilize the angels to Scripture alone.

ACTIVITY OF ANGELS

As a prominent principal doctrine in God's Word, these heralds of heaven are found in Genesis, Exodus, Numbers, Joshua, Judges and throughout the Bible. They are positioned in the pages all the way to Revelation.

As we will discover, the array of angels specified in Scripture range in rank. There are seraphim, cherubim, archangels, living creatures, powers, horses of fire, chariots of fire, ministering spirits and angels which appear in the form of man.

Adding these references together, you will find a Bible filled with angelic activity in heaven and on earth. To eliminate angels is to deny the *providence*, *provision* and *protection* of the hand of heaven to you.

Angels are not spoken of once or twice, but literally hundreds of times in God's Word.

SERVANTS OF THE SON

Beloved reader, I first want to establish that angels are not to be *worshiped.* They were created by the Lord and are subservient subjects in His Kingdom.

Jesus Christ is the Pre-existent, Self-existent Eternal Lord who became flesh for our sake (John 1:1-3,14). Scripture declares: *"For by him were all things created, that are in heaven, and that are in earth, visible and invisible, whether they be thrones, or dominions, or principalities, or powers: all things were created by him, and for him"* (Colossians 1:16).

God's Word tells us, *"...when he bringeth in the*

13

firstbegotten into the world, he saith, And let all the angels of God worship him. And of the angels he saith, Who maketh his angels spirits, and his ministers a flame of fire. But unto the Son he saith, Thy throne, O God, is for ever and ever: a sceptre of righteousness is the sceptre of thy kingdom" (Hebrews 1:6-8).

There is no question that Jesus Christ is the Creator and King of all angels (John 1:3, 10).

His servants and their orders come as commanded from Him: *"But to which of the angels said he at any time, Sit on my right hand, until I make thine enemies thy footstool?"* (v.13). He has placed *"...all things under his feet"* (Ephesians 1:22).

In John's revelation, thousands and thousands of angels are around the throne paying their homage to Him alone (Revelation 5).

For this reason, we never bow to any angels, only to Jesus Christ, the Eternal Word. As the psalmist writes, *"Bless the Lord, ye his angels, that excel in*

14

strength, that do his commandments, hearkening unto the voice of his word" (Psalm 103:20).

THE CREATION AND FORMATION OF ANGELS

Genesis 1 unfolds evidence angels were brought into existence on the first day of creation.

"In the beginning God created the heaven and the earth" (Genesis 1:1). This text not only speaks of earth, but heaven itself—which was created first because Scripture mentions it first.

Continuing in the context, God said, *"Let there be light..."*(v.3). We know the Lord was not speaking of physical light as we understand it on earth. The light we enjoy comes from the sun and the moon.

The luminaries of this light were created on the fourth day (vv.14-19). *"And God said, Let there be lights in the firmament of the heaven to divide the day from the night; and let them be for signs, and for seasons, and for days, and years" "And the evening and the morning were the fourth day"*(v.19).

It was only after the light from the sun and the

15

moon were spoken into existence that time as we know it was created.

Only after the fourth day of creation did we have the ability to measure moments of time in 24-hour periods.

Remember, Scripture is infallible and inerrant. Therefore, this ends the argument over the presumed age of the earth being in contradiction to the Bible. The earth can be millions, even billions of years old since it was created on the third day—before time was introduced on the fourth day.

After scrutinizing Scripture, there is a decipherable difference between the light created on the first day and the "lights" and luminaries of the fourth day.

May I take you deeper?

THE FATEFUL FALL
OF THE MASTER MUSICIAN

What does Scripture tell us about the fateful fall of one who was once a beautiful cherub, but is now called the devil?

Some have mistakenly misunderstood the devil was

a fallen archangel, but beloved, the enemy of your soul was not the anthesis of Michael the archangel.

[handwritten: direct opposite]

———— ∽ ————

The adversary was at one time the anointed cherubim—the chieftain of the cherubim.

[handwritten: Leader]

In Ezekiel we read, *"Thou art the anointed cherub that covereth; and I have set thee so: thou wast upon the holy mountain of God; thou hast walked up and down in the midst of the stones of fire"* (Ezekiel 18:14).

Then we learn, ***"Thou wast perfect in thy ways from the day that thou wast created, till iniquity was found in thee"*** (v.15). And God said, *"Thine heart was lifted up because of thy beauty, thou hast corrupted thy wisdom by reason of thy brightness"* (v.17).

Satan was the musician over the majesty of God. In the holiest of holies in heaven he covered and hovered over the exalted throne of God. As Scripture records, *"...the workmanship of thy tabrets and of thy pipes was prepared in thee in the day that thou wast*

17

created" (v.13). This was the *"...the anointed cherub that covereth"*(v.14).

According to the words the Lord spoke through Ezekiel, in one moment the master musician used his position in revolt and rebellion against God.

Satan was an annointed Chieftain → Cherub

Pride, jealousy, covetousness and vanity denote a personality with elements of emotion.

His imagination of pride

Ezekiel portrays and conveys the anointed cherub was given a choice. He was created with a rational soul and sense. But through self-conceit, he consigned his deceit into a fatal fall forever.

The text in Isaiah teaches how his beauty became brazen: *"For thou hast said in thine heart, I will ascend into heaven, I will exalt my throne above the stars of God: I will sit also upon the mount of the congregation, in the sides of the north: I will ascend above the heights of the clouds; I will be like the most High"* (Isaiah 14:13-14).

It was these imaginations of pride that became the

root of all rebellion and sin.

THE GUARD OF THE GARDEN

The first mention of angels in Scripture involves the aftermath of the fall of man. Adam was originally placed in the garden, "*...to dress it and to keep it*" before he was driven from his destiny (Genesis 2:15).

In Hebrew, the verb "to dress" is *abad*—meaning labor. And the word "keep" is *shamar*—to guard.

———— ∼ ————

Adam's ministry is a prophetic preview of priesthood.

According to Genesis 2:15, he was called to serve and to guard the garden. Since his assignment was to "dress and keep it," he was designated to protect the presence of God.

Eden was the first tabernacle on earth because it was where the presence came down each day (Genesis 3:8).

19

The trees were spiritual trees: *"...the tree of knowledge of good and evil"* (Genesis 2:9) and *"...the tree of life also in the midst of the garden"* (v.9),

When Adam sinned, he entered into exile —distanced from his destiny. It was now necessary for God to replace the ministry of protecting the presence and guarding the glory.

Who did He dispatch? Scripture tells us angels were sent into the sanctuary on earth—Eden. *"So he drove out the man; and he placed at the east of the garden of Eden Cherubims, and a flaming sword which turned every way, to keep the way of the tree of life"* (Genesis 3:24).

This verse authenticates and demonstrates our highest purpose is priesthood.

"ANGELS UNAWARES"
THE SAINT'S SECRET SERVICE

Be not forgetful to entertain strangers: for thereby some have entertained angels unawares.

– HEBREWS 13:2

Angels are invisible, secret agents of God's assistance to you—the hands of heaven extended to earth for your welfare and warfare. *"For he shall give his angels charge over thee, to keep thee in all thy ways"* (Psalm 91:11).

What do we mean by "secret service to the saints"? As the writer of Hebrews says, we have often "entertained angels unawares."

The Greek word for "unawares" is *lanthano* —which means to "lie hidden." This being the case, angels are often unseen as they dispense help from heaven on their assignment to you. However, sometimes they are disguised in the form of men.

THE ROAD TO REBEKAH

When Abraham was old and his son, Isaac, still wasn't married, he called for Eliezer, his trusted servant to, *"...go unto my country, and to my kindred, and take a wife unto my son Isaac"* (Genesis 24:4).

Eliezer questioned, "But what if the woman refuses to leave and come back with me?"

Abraham told him not to worry, *"...he shall send*

his angel before thee, and thou shalt take a wife unto my son from thence" (v.7).

With total trust, Abraham believed God's angel would direct Eliezer into the path of providence designed for the future destiny of his people.

Just as the Lord planned, the angel led the servant to Rebekah, who became Isaac's wife.

A "MAN OF MACEDONIA"

The ministry of "angels unawares" can even come to you while you are sleeping.

Perhaps you have had a dream where you recognized most of the "players," yet the identity of one person was unclear. Maybe the individual looked like someone you once knew, but you were not sure.

If that person clarified or confirmed a message which came in the dream, it could be an "angel unawares" sent by heaven to give you divine direction.

This happened to the apostle Paul.

After experiencing an excruciating split with his companion in ministry, Barnabas, Paul was at a crossroads.

Venturing forward to fulfill God's will, he set sail for Galatia when the Holy Spirit stopped him twice and rerouted his direction.

The apostle was weary, not knowing which way to turn when, suddenly, "...*a vision appeared to Paul in the night; There stood a man of Macedonia, and prayed him, saying, Come over into Macedonia, and help us. And after he had seen the vision, immediately we endeavoured to go into Macedonia, assuredly gathering that the Lord had called us for to preach the gospel unto them*" (Acts 16:9-10).

Personally, I believe the unknown man in the dream was an "angel unawares" sent to Paul to direct him in the perfect plan and purpose of the Father.

ANGELS AND PERSEVERANCE IN PRAYER

You may ask, "How can I access and appropriate my covenant rights concerning angels assigned to me?"

23

―――― ⟿ ――――

*One of the ways these agents of
God are dispatched and designated
is through the power of prayer.*

When Jerusalem was in ruins, Daniel sought the Lord for an answer—and God sent an angel. Scripture records, *"Yea, whiles I was speaking in prayer, even the man Gabriel, whom I had seen in the vision at the beginning, being caused to fly swiftly, touched me about the time of the evening oblation. And he informed me, and talked with me, and said, O Daniel, I am now come forth to give thee skill and understanding. At the beginning of thy supplications the commandment came forth, and I am come to show thee; for thou art greatly beloved: therefore understand the matter, and consider the vision"* (Daniel 9:21-23).

At his time of need—while deep in supplication—the Lord sent the angel Gabriel with exactly the answer Daniel needed. He was given precise details regarding how Jerusalem would be restored.

ANGELIC CARE AND COMFORT

Perseverance in prayer facilitates and appropriates angels on their "secret service" mission.

Peter the apostle experienced this when Herod was persecuting leaders of the early church. He was arrested, put in prison, but while he was behind bars, *"...prayer was made without ceasing of the church unto God for him"* (Acts 12:5).

Here was Peter, sleeping between two soldiers, bound by chains and being watched by the warden.

What Herod's guards didn't understand was the awesome power of prayer. Suddenly, while the believers were pleading "unto God" on Peter's behalf, the Lord dispatched an angelic messenger on a secret, heavenly assignment. *"And, behold, the angel of the Lord came upon him, and a light shined in the prison: and he smote Peter on the side, and raised him up, saying, Arise up quickly. And his chains fell off from his hands"* (v.7).

The contexts clearly verifies and clarifies the power of prayer.

25

———— ∾ ————

The miraculous ministry of the angel dispatched for Peter's deliverance was a direct result of a praying body of believers.

Peter thought he was dreaming, not knowing it was truly a messenger of God. *"And the angel said unto him, Gird thyself, and bind on thy sandals. And so he did. And he saith unto him, Cast thy garment about thee, and follow me"* (v.8).

Swiftly, they made their way to the iron gates which led out into the street and the angel departed. Only then did Peter come to himself and realize, *"Now I know of a surety, that the Lord hath sent his angel, and hath delivered me out of the hand of Herod"* (v.11).

God's "secret service" to Peter included the compassion and care of a loving Father—even to making sure his shoes were fastened and there was a garment to keep him warm. The Lord orchestrated and coordinated every aspect of the apostle's deliverance.

ATTENDING AND DEFENDING

Like Daniel and Peter, you are guarded and protected. Because you belong to Him, "angels unawares" are assigned to attend and defend you wherever you go.

Jesus, I thank You for the blood-bought privilege of angels assigned to me. I claim my full covenant rights as Your child.

Release "angels unawares" over my family, my health, my business affairs, my dreams and my destiny. Protect and direct me in the path of Your providence through the secret service of Your angels.

Amen.

27

CHAPTER TWO

THE ARCHANGEL AND HIS ARMIES

And there was war in heaven:
Michael and his angels fought against
the dragon; and the dragon fought and his
angels, and [they] *prevailed not..."*

– REVELATION 12:7-8

Heavenly hosts are spiritually strategized in a defined design for battle.

In Revelation 12, the militant myriads are columned for combat with Michael at the helm of the hosts. And according to Daniel 10:21 and 12:1, he is the chief warrior who wages war in the heavenlies.

Did you know these angelic armies are assigned to

battle for your breakthrough as you take territory for the Kingdom? Please allow me to take you deeper into the depths of His Word.

First, we must understand no angel wages war without an order of obedience from the Word of God. As the psalmist writes, *"Bless the Lord, ye his angels, that excel in strength, that do his commandments, hearkening unto the voice of his word"* (Psalm 103:20).

THE REALMS AND RANKS OF THE ANGELIC ARMIES

The apostle Paul classifies the realms and ranks of the angelic armies into four categories. The listed legions are:

1. Thrones.
2. Dominions.
3. Principalities.
4, Powers.

"For by him were all things created, that are in

heaven, and that are in earth, visible and invisible, whether they be thrones, or dominions, or principalities, or powers: all things were created by him, and for him" (Colossians 1:16).

Scripture does not reveal many of the names of angels, however Michael is mentioned as the commander and chief of the heavenly hosts. In fact, the Hebrew interpretation of the name Michael is "Who is like God?"

Even in his name he points praises to the only Worthy one—Jesus Christ.

A REGIMENT FOR RULERSHIP

All rule in heaven and earth is under the sovereign regimen of Jesus as the King of kings and Lord of lords (1 Timothy 6:15).

In order to execute the excellency of His glory, the angelic armies are positioned in place to propel His power on behalf of His command.

31

In Scripture we are given two decipherable divisions of Michael's position of power for the glory of God:

FIRST:
MICHAEL WAGES WAR AGAINST PRINCIPALITIES AND POWERS

"For we wrestle not against flesh and blood, but against principalities, against powers, against the rulers of the darkness of this world, against spiritual wickedness in high places" (Ephesians 6:12).

What does this mean—and how does this involve the angelic armies on your behalf?

Scripture gives us evidence that prayer, supplication, fasting and focus toward the promises of God catapult our prayers into a new level of anointing.

Humbling ourselves before the Lord in such ongoing intercession releases the help of the heavenly hosts for us. It is especially powerful when we are prompted by the promises in His Word and are willing to fight the good fight by faith.

This is exactly what happened to Daniel as he

sought answers from God. *"In those days I Daniel was mourning three full weeks. In those days I Daniel was mourning three full weeks. I ate no pleasant bread, neither came flesh nor wine in my mouth, neither did I anoint myself at all, till three whole weeks were fulfilled"* (Daniel 10:2-3).

After 21 days of seeking by strong supplication, an angel revealed something strategic to Daniel.

His prayers released a war in the heavenlies with victory for God's people.

YOUR POSITION IN PRAYER

Michael, called the "chief prince," was dispatched to withstand in war during these three weeks against the wicked powers which had held God's people captive: *"Then said he unto me, Fear not, Daniel: for from the first day that thou didst set thine heart to understand, and to chasten thyself before thy God, thy*

33

words were heard, and I am come for thy words. But the prince of the kingdom of Persia withstood me one and twenty days: but, lo, Michael, one of the chief princes, came to help me..."(Daniel 10:12-13).

Your prayer life positions and releases the angels to wage war on your behalf. *"I Daniel understood by books the number of the years, whereof the word of the Lord came to Jeremiah the prophet..."*(Daniel 9:2).

Please notice how his prayer was prompted by the Word. Then he continued, *"And I set my face unto the Lord God, to seek by prayer and supplications, with fasting, and sackcloth, and ashes..."* (v.3).

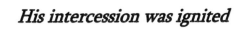

**His intercession was ignited
by fasting and the forces of faith.**

Daniel stretched in his consecration and separation unto God.

Scripture articulates and punctuates how Gabriel —another archangel—was caused by God to come to Daniel's aid because of his constant, relentless combat in prayer (v.21). *"At the beginning of thy supplications the commandment came forth"* (v.23).

A merciful God brought the aid and answer by dispatching His angel to Daniel. Why? Because he was in prayer and supplication—beseeching the Lord.

ANGELIC ASSISTANCE

Continuing in the context of verse 21, the text teaches it was the uninterrupted faithfulness of ongoing prayer and fasting which allowed Daniel to receive a revelation.

This is not dead history, but is personal, powerful, prophetic and applicable NOW in your life!

The Bible tells us, *"Yea, while I was speaking in prayer, even the man Gabriel, whom I had seen in the vision at the beginning, being caused to fly swiftly..."* (v.21).

Beloved, please understand the objective of Scripture is not so we communicate with angels, but that the merciful God will disperse them to assist us through fasting and prayer.

SECOND:
MICHAEL IS THE PRINCE OF THE
HEAVENLY HOST ASSIGNED TO
PROTECT GOD'S ELECT AGAINST THE
ACCUSING ADVERSARY.

Daniel prayed, *"...there is none that holdeth with me in these things, but Michael your prince"* (Daniel 10:21).

Michael is the archangel who stands and commands the battle on behalf of Israel—and spiritual Israel, the church. This is why Scripture specifies "Michael your prince."

The text designates a provision made concerning and precisely *for* Israel on behalf of a merciful Lord.

Daniel 12 teaches the ministry of Michael will be especially employed and deployed in the last days. Again, the emphasis is on the defense of Israel, and spiritual Israel, the church. *"And at that time shall Michael stand up, the great prince which standeth for the children of thy people..."* (Daniel 12:1).

Revelation reveals his militant myriads engaged in combat to cast down the accuser in the heavenlies.

This war brings great glory to the name of Jesus.

The Bible tells us, *"And there was war in heaven: Michael and his angels fought against the dragon; and the dragon fought and his angels, And prevailed not; neither was their place found any more in heaven. And the great dragon was cast out, that old serpent, called the Devil, and Satan, which deceiveth the whole world: he was cast out into the earth, and his angels were cast out with him. And I heard a loud voice saying in heaven, Now is come salvation, and strength, and the kingdom of our God, and the power of his Christ: for the accuser of our brethren is cast down, which accused them before our God day and night"* (Revelation 12:7-10).

Beloved, because of the blood of Jesus there is no weapon formed against you that can prosper (Isaiah 54:17).

Satan

No longer can your familiar foe legally accuse you before God.

CHRIST THE CHAMPION

Because of the ultimate sacrifice on Calvary's cross, the accuser has absolutely no place or position against you. This means you stand in the righteousness of God in Christ.

Jesus conquerors him and is the Champion against all principalities and powers (Colossians 2:15).

———— ∼ ————

Christ is the Mighty Warrior who has won the war for you as a believer.

Purchased by the price of Calvary, He has assigned Michael to do battle against all accusations of the adversary against you. *"Yet Michael the archangel, when contending with the devil he disputed about the body of Moses, durst not bring against him a railing accusation, but said, The Lord rebuke thee"* (Jude 1:9).

Thank God, we are not fighting the battle alone!

Lord Jesus, I praise You as the Champion of

my warfare. I receive an anointing by faith to enter into a greater consecration and separation to take the territory You promised me. With confidence in the cross, and assurance by the blood, I ask you to disperse the heavenly hosts to wage war for

_____.

(Your prayer request)

Thank You for the angels You assign—not only for my welfare, but also for my warfare. Amen.

39

CHAPTER THREE

ESCORTED BY AN EXTRAORDINARY ENTOURAGE

For he shall give his angels charge
over thee, to keep thee in all thy ways. They
shall bear thee up in their hands, lest thou
dash thy foot against a stone.

– PSALM 91:11-12

*D*id you know you are so valuable to God that He sends a heavenly entourage to escort you on your life's journey?

His Word promises He has angels specifically assigned to guard and guide you here on earth. These are special heavenly beings who protect the elect and belong to the angelic category classified in Scripture as "the angel of the Lord."

Unlike the six-winged seraphim or the four-winged cherubim mentioned in God's Word, they are the two-winged angels who provide providence and protection for believers.

The Bible teaches that these angels on assignment are a product of the security Jesus purchased on Calvary's cross. *"Are they not all ministering spirits, sent forth to minister for them who shall be heirs of salvation?"* (Hebrews 1:14).

DIVINE DELIVERANCE

Perhaps you have had a near-death experience and wondered, "How did I escape?" Never forget, *"The angel of the Lord encampeth round about them that fear him, and delivereth them"* (Psalm 34:7).

I pray this chapter will provide comfort concerning your personal safety—and the protection of those you love. You can experience the "caress" of God through His angels appointed to you.

IN THEIR HANDS THEY HOLD YOU

Scripture is sensitive to those who face the fear of the unknown—and God is not cold or calloused toward what is difficult in your life.

When the Word addresses what is excruciating or debilitating, the text both validates your pain and renders reliance on the Father. As the psalmist writes, *"Yea, though I walk through the valley of the shadow of death, I will fear no evil: for thou art with me; thy rod and thy staff they comfort me"* (Psalm 23:4).

The Lord is saying, "There are secrets under the surface—deep down in your heart—which are precious to Me." It is for this very reason He has placed "heavenly custodians" over you for provision and care.

Your life is entrusted into the hands of these angelic escorts and the Bible assures us, *"He that dwelleth in the secret place of the most High shall abide under the shadow of the Almighty"* (Psalm 91:1).

43

————— ∽ —————

This "shadow" is the extension of His presence from heaven to earth.

PROTECTION AND DIRECTION

Though God is everywhere because He is the Omnipresent One (Psalm 139:8), those who abide in Him dwell in this "secret place"—and angels are the agents hidden in His shadow.

Be assured, *"He shall cover thee with his feathers, and under his wings shalt thou trust: his truth shall be thy shield and buckler"* (Psalm 91:4).

————— ∽ —————

God promises His protection will bring direction to lead you out of danger and into your destiny.

Remember, *"...he shall give his angels charge over thee, to keep thee in all thy ways"* (Psalm 91:11). This means He will not only shelter you, but provide guidance.

Because you are covered by the covenant, angels are delegated to place you in strategic positions for those miraculous moments which are aligned with God's plan for your future: *"They shall bear thee up in their hands, lest thou dash thy foot against a stone"* (Psalm 91:12).

THE COMMISSION OF THEIR MISSION IS YOUR WELFARE AND WARFARE

In David's psalms we learn how angels not only attend but also *defend* those allied in covenant. These representatives of the Lord have been delegated and dedicated to bring a breakthrough in your battle.

They are assigned to assist you and also persist against the wiles of the wicked one. *"Let them be as chaff before the wind: and let the angel of the Lord chase them. Let their way be dark and slippery: and let the angel of the Lord persecute them"* (Psalm 35:5-6).

This means heaven shares, and also *bears,* the

45

battle on your behalf. Angels are waging war and defending everything which concerns you.

GOD'S AGENTS OF
RESTORATION AND CONSOLATION

The Abrahamic covenant is the first place in Scripture we can trace angels on an assignment to individual people on earth in the form of men. The first angels, however, were the cherubim in the Garden of Eden.

One of the truly remarkable threads in the fabric of Scripture is how God uses His angels to protect the covenant He has made with man.

Especially relevant to you and your household is the divine agreement the Lord entered into with His servant Abraham—who stands alone in Hebrew Scripture as one who pleased God by his righteousness and great faith.

It was a covenant of incredible promise and tremendous blessing, not only for Abraham, but for the future of all humanity.

This pact began with God's great call and

commission: *"Now the Lord had said unto Abram, Get thee out of thy country, and from thy kindred, and from thy father's house, unto a land that I will show thee: And I will make of thee a great nation, and I will bless thee, and make thy name great; and thou shalt be a blessing: And I will bless them that bless thee, and curse him that curseth thee: and in thee shall all families of the earth be blessed"* (Genesis 12:1-3).

A BELIEVER'S BLOODLINE

By asking Abraham to leave his father's house, his native country and all he ever knew, God was preparing him for Himself, consecrating him for the unique purpose for which he had been created.

Through this important covenant, Abraham's bloodline was divinely ordained to be the conduit through which redemption would come to the whole world.

47

God, in His faithfulness, fulfilled His Word —His promised seed to Abraham is Jesus Christ (Galatians 3:16).

This is so momentous that, after Jehovah God first makes the promise we have just read, and the one found in Genesis 13:14-17, He formalizes them in a covenant (Genesis 15:18-21).

To further emphasize the significance of this unique agreement, He repeats His covenant four more times in Scripture to Abraham and his descendants, Isaac and Jacob (Genesis 17:6-8; 22:16-18; 26:3-4; 28:13-14).

However, God's Word does not limit the definition of the descendants of Abraham to just a physical lineage, but also to his spiritual bloodline.

RESCUED FROM THE RUINS

From the Word, let me show you how God uses angels to protect this covenant.

In the household of Abraham was a women named Hagar, an Egyptian princess and a daughter of

Pharaoh. She was given as a maidservant to Abraham's wife, Sarah, in Egypt because Pharaoh saw the miracles God performed on behalf of Sarah (Genesis 12:17).

On their return to Canaan, since Sarah was unable to bear children, she suggested Abraham father a child with Hagar (Genesis 16:2).

Her pregnancy resulted in a great conflict between Sarah, and Hagar (v.7) and the maid became arrogant and insolent to her mistress, forgetting her subordinate position. Sarah, however, continued to treat the woman according to her role as a servant.

For Hagar, this was intolerable. Unable to cope with her mixed feelings—and the pain which was part of her pregnancy—she ran away from home, fleeing into the wilderness.

Hagar prophetically prefigures those who have misdirected, disconnected emotions.

She could only hope she would survive the

incredibly difficult journey back to Egypt. Uncertain, desperate, and very alone, she found a well in the desert and, exhausted, stopped to rest.

DELIVERANCE IN THE DESERT

Abraham was the patriarch of loving-kindness and his righteous heart surely ached for Hagar to return. However, out of deep respect for his wife Sarah, he did not interfere or send after Hagar to have her brought back.

But remember, God made a covenant with Abraham which extended even to Hagar as a member of his household. In this situation, a call went out from heaven and an angel was quickly dispatched with an assignment to rescue the maidservant and restore her to her place of destiny.

At the lowest ebb of her despair,
resting by the well in that vast wasteland,
a glorious angel of the Lord revealed
the plan of God to Hagar.

Even though she was a pagan Egyptian, she was now part of Abraham's household, and God had a predestined purpose for her.

The angel asked, "What are you doing here?"

Hagar answered, *"I flee from the face of my mistress Sarai"* (v.8).

The angel of the Lord continued, *"Return to thy mistress, and submit thyself under her hands...*[and] *I will multiply thy seed exceedingly, that it shall not be numbered for multitude"* (v.10).

If the God of Abraham, in His faithfulness, sought out Hagar by sending His angel, will He not do the same for you?

In order to communicate that God's faithfulness extended to Abraham's household by sending angelic assistance, Scripture documents the details with the story of Hagar.

There is also mercy in this message for you.

In Abraham's anguish, angels were assigned even over his servant because she was carrying his child. The angels were God's agents of restoration.

RETURN AND REPENT!

God, in His infinite wisdom, waited by the well for Hagar. When she had reached the end of herself, she was finally ready for her divine visitation: to hear what God wanted to say. The Lord was prepared to rebuild the ruins of her life and lift her into the purpose for which she had been created.

When she stopped for a drink at the well, it tells us prophetically she was also seeking refreshment from the water (the anointing) of God's Spirit. Only when she was ready to receive did the angel appear.

In Hebrew, the idea of "return" encompasses a much broader concept than in English. It is *tshuvah*—meaning not only a physical return; it also implies repentance.

PREGNANT WITH A PROMISE

The angel told Hagar, *"Behold, thou art with child, and shalt bear a son, and shalt call his name Ishmael; because the Lord hath heard thy affliction"*(vv.10-11).

Hagar was rescued out of the ruins of dilemma and disappointment. God sent an angel in search of her because she belonged to Abraham—one of His own because of the covenant.

In a personal sense of Scripture, Hagar prophetically

parallels those who are in pain yet giving birth to God's promise.

HELD BY HEAVENLY HANDS

Precious child of God, when you cannot cope with your calamity and your life crumbles into disarray, please know that you are pregnant with the promise of God for your life.

Later we will discuss the types and species of angels, but this is the first time Scripture makes reference to an "angel of the Lord"—a two-winged creature (the cherubim mentioned in the Garden of Eden had four wings; the seraphim in Isaiah 6 have six wings).

This is significant since it was soon after God made His covenant with the "father of nations," that He releases an angel of the Lord to directly intervene in the affairs of Abraham's family.

Even more important, every time an angel of the Lord appears, it is solely in response to the Abrahamic covenant—whether in the Hebrew scriptures, the New

Testament or in God's continuing ministry to His people today.

———— ∾ ————

As God sent His angel to watch over the Word He placed in Hagar, so will He send them to protect the prophecy over your life.

When you feel hopeless, heaven sends help in the form of heavenly beings. In their hands they hold you and from the storms they shelter you.

PROTECTION FOR THE PRODIGAL

Perhaps you are in spiritual warfare for the welfare of your son, daughter or loved one and are critically concerned for your family. It may involve a disastrous relationship or the behavior of a child which has gripped your heart with grief.

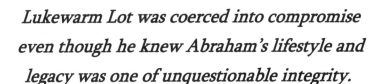

Lukewarm Lot was coerced into compromise even though he knew Abraham's lifestyle and legacy was one of unquestionable integrity.

The Bible records that wherever Abraham journeyed, his nephew accompanied him (Genesis 11:31; 12:4-5; 13:1).

Despite all the years of learning and living with his righteous uncle, Lot was still strongly influenced by his former lifestyle in Haran.

Deceived by his own double-mindedness, Lot moved out of protection into peril.

He found himself living a compromised life outside of the security of Abraham's tent. Lot had chosen to reside in a land which appeared to be prosperous, though in fact was dead and decaying. The cities of two kingdoms already occupied that valley—Sodom and Gomorrah.

Scripture tells us, *"...the men of Sodom were wicked and sinners before the Lord exceedingly"* (v.13).

DESCENT INTO DEGENERACY

We learn from the rabbis how the citizens of Sodom were so utterly depraved they made it illegal to be hospitable to strangers. Instead, it was required for residents to perpetrate hateful and lustful acts upon visitors to their town, to prevent others from enjoying the supposed richness of the fertile valley. Any who showed hospitality were put to death!

Through the unwise choices he made, Lot quickly found himself ensnared in the sin and darkness of Sodom and Gomorrah.

Even though 2 Peter 2:7-8 calls Lot a righteous and just man, he was not immune to the powerful temptations of iniquity, greed and pride. However, Lot's descent into degeneracy was not instantaneous; rather a result of a gradual, progressive decline.

He *"...pitched his tent toward Sodom"* (Genesis 13:12).

DELIVERANCE FROM DEGRADATION

When the Lord visited Abraham through angels in

Genesis 18 after announcing Sarah would have a son, God also pronounced judgment on the cities of Sodom and Gomorrah.

As a result of God's secret, revealed to His servant Abraham, concerning the impending judgment on these wicked communities, Abraham begins to cry out with a heart of compassion for the city's inhabitants, and also Lot.

God's mercy was immediately dispersed as He dispatched angels to deliver Lot before there was calamity and catastrophe. The Bible records, *"And there came two angels to Sodom at even; and Lot sat in the gate of Sodom: and Lot seeing them rose up to meet them; and he bowed himself with his face toward the ground"* (Genesis 19:1).

Scripture does not detail these events just to give you a history of the Hebrews.

In the passages we learn of the power of a covenant which comes as protection even for a prodigal.

The objective is Scripture is not just so we can capture the chronology of historical events. In the context is a concise message which is personal, prophetic and relevant for us today.

It is a word of hope to those who are weary and worn from weeping over their sons, daughters and loved ones—crying for them to be protected and directed by heaven.

Because you are travailing, God's power is *availing*, with angels assigned to the ones you hold dear.

GOD'S ANGELS AT THE GATE

Beloved, no matter how far our loved ones may have fallen and regardless how hopeless their situation seems, God still wants us to intercede with Him on their behalf.

The Lord heard and honored Abraham's prayer and said, "Even though Lot is living in sin, My covenant with Abraham is so strong, before I destroy Sodom and Gomorrah, I am going to deliver Lot and his family out of that evil place."

Sitting at the gate of Sodom meant Lot had so declined into demented thinking he became an "elder" judge at the gate. The biblical pattern for "sitting at the gate" as referring to an elder is found in the life of Mordecai who sat at the gates of Shushan (Esther 2) and Boaz at the gates in Bethlehem (Ruth 4).

CALLED BY THE COVENANT"

The angels said to Lot, *"...whatsoever thou hast in the city, bring them out....For we will destroy this place, because the cry of them is waxen great before the face of the Lord; and the Lord hath sent us to destroy it"* (Genesis 19:12-13).

As the sun came up the next morning, the angels commanded Lot, *"Arise, take thy wife, and thy two daughters, which are here; lest thou be consumed in the iniquity of the city. And while he lingered, the men laid hold upon his hand, and upon the hand of his wife, and upon the hand of his two daughters; the Lord being merciful unto him: and they brought him forth, and set him without the city"* (vv.15-16).

The Lord pleaded, *"...haste thee, escape thither; for I cannot do any thing till thou be come thither"* (v.22). *"And it came to pass, when God destroyed the cities of the plain, that God remembered Abraham, and sent Lot out of the midst of the overthrow, when he overthrew the cities in the which Lot dwelt"* (v.29).

WATCHING THE WAYWARD

If God protected Abraham's family, how much more will He do for you who have been bought by the blood of Jesus?

Please know even the slightest sigh or whisper of a loved one is heard by God.

Both Hagar and Lot received deliverance because they were connected to Abraham. And just as they were rescued, so will the Father watch over the wayward members of your family.

Lot and Hagar prophetically prefigure how He assigns angels to those who have wandered down a wayward path.

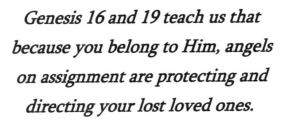

Genesis 16 and 19 teach us that because you belong to Him, angels on assignment are protecting and directing your lost loved ones.

Let me share how the Lord caused this to be real in my life.

I will never forget the first time I stepped into a pulpit to teach and preach. After seven years of training, on February 20, 1977, the day finally arrived—and the location was over 150 miles one way from our home.

It was about 1:30 in the morning when I arrived back in Brea, California, still rejoicing and praising the Lord for allowing me to minister that night.

As I was driving up Date Street, I noticed an automobile coming toward me—yet it seemed to be strangely covered in what I can only describe as a "gold fog."

As, I drove closer, the gold took on the shape of wings which spread out over the car. Immediately, I knew God was showing me something supernatural and I wondered, "Whose car is this?"

My mind thought about believers who lived nearby. Could it be Reverend McFadden, the Baptist preacher who lives down the street—or his son? Was it the Morrisons, our neighbors since childhood? I pondered, "They love the Lord so deeply and this is God's presence over their car."

However, as the vehicle approached, I could see it was an old, white Volkswagen van, driven by my younger brother—who at the time was living contrary to God's call on his life.

This was one of the few visions I have ever seen. It was the Lord showing me He had sent His mighty angel to watch over my brother.

In my mind it would seem only logical for God to send an angel, like a golden mist, over the car of someone deeply spiritual. So seeing the van and recognizing it was my wayward brother, both shocked and surprised me.

In retrospect, I realize it was the hand of heaven protecting the prodigal with His angels.

"CROSSING THE CAMPS"

We can learn more concerning how God sends His heavenly entourage to escort you by reading Genesis 32. *"And Jacob went on his way, and the angels of God met him. And when Jacob saw them, he said, This is God's host: and he called the name of that place Mahanaim"* (Genesis 32:1-2).

In a literal sense of Scripture, the word "Mahanaim" is translated, "crossing the camps."

This means one band of angels led Jacob to the borders of Haran, and the other band met him at the crossing into the land of Canaan. Literally there were two separate encampments, and when he passed over the borders of one land to another, he "crossed the camps" of the angels.

Remember, as Abraham's grandson, Jacob was covered by the covenant. This heavenly entourage not only escorted him safely, they directed him into his destiny.

Crossing the camps also teaches us the angels assisted and awaited Jacob as he neared the borders. I believe this was necessary because there were barriers at the boundaries in the realm of the Spirit.

The opposition wanted to block Jacob from entering into Israel, the land of his promise. But God in His faithfulness sent angel bands—escorting him past the blockades into the land of Canaan.

God also promises you a "Mahanaim" experience.

Are you about to cross camps into a new career or entering a new phase of your life? Genesis 32 is a personal and prophetic word for you.

God has His angels waiting as you cross the borders into your future.

There is no need to feel uncertain when His hands from heaven, in the form of heavenly creatures, are waiting to guide you.

Let me ask you to pray this prayer with me:

Dear Jesus, I thank you that I am escorted by a heavenly entourage. I claim Genesis 32 and am thankful Your bands of angels are awaiting me at the borders.

I ask You to send them to direct me into my destiny. Command them, O Lord, to break the barriers which are blocking my future.

Amen.

CHAPTER FOUR

THE SANCTUARY OF THE SERAPHIM

Above it stood the seraphims: each
one had six wings; with twain he covered
his face, and with twain he covered his
feet, and with twain he did fly.

— ISAIAH 6:2

There is a special classification of angels which have never appeared on earth—only in a vision. They are six-winged creatures called seraphim.

As we will see, it is the eternal assignment of the seraphim to be near the altar of God in heaven, revealing the holiness of the Almighty, and conveying His glory through their words and actions.

However, their existence means something more. In the sanctuary of the seraphim the holiness of heaven can be conceptualized and visualized through the tabernacle in the wilderness—the habitation of heaven on earth.

A PATTERN OF PERFECTION

The details of the tabernacle were given by divine design to Moses at Mount Sinai during his third 40-day fast. God said, *"And look that thou make them after their pattern, which was showed thee in the mount"* (Exodus 25:40).

Scripture synchronizes the pattern in heaven which was to be made visual on earth—a reflection of God's perfection.

As the Word declares, the Lord shows us an *"...example and shadow of heavenly things, as Moses was admonished of God when he was about to make* the tabernacle: for, See, saith he, that thou make all things according to the pattern showed to thee in the mount" (Hebrews 8:5).

King David also received the temple blueprints as a divine design harmonizing with heaven "And the pattern of all that he had by the spirit, of the courts of the house of the Lord..." (1 Chronicles 28:12). "And for the altar of incense refined gold by weight; and gold for the pattern of the chariot of the cherubims, that spread out their wings, and covered the ark of the covenant of the Lord. All this, said David, the Lord **made me understand** in writing by his hand upon me, even all the works of this pattern" (vv.18-19).

A GLIMPSE OF GLORY

Throughout Scripture, using the tabernacle and the temple there are prophetic parallels that give us an insight of what heaven is like. For example, in heaven as on earth:

- There is an ark (Revelation 11:19).

69

- There is a menorah with seven candlesticks—or branches (Revelation 1:13).
- There is the golden altar of incense (Revelation 8:3).
- There are golden censers (v.8).
- The place of His presence is called the temple (Revelation 11:1-2,19).

As John was allowed to see heaven, he writes, *"...I looked, and, behold, the temple of the tabernacle of the testimony in heaven was opened...And the temple was filled with smoke from the glory of God"* (Revelation 15:5,8).

It is through understanding the splendor of these similarities we are able to define and align the sanctuary of the seraphim.

TEARS AROUND THE THRONE

Unlike other angels, the six-winged seraphim never leave the parameters of their heavenly paradise.

Cherubim and archangels are different, since they

descend to earth. In Ezekiel they are described as chariots of God's glory which carry the presence of the Almighty between earth and heaven (Ezekiel 1; 9:3; 10:4; 10:22-23).

Also, the hosts of archangels (princes) are commissioned to combat in the heavenlies outside the borders of heaven (Daniel 10:13,21; 12:1).

The seraphim, however, are paradigms of unending praise—always positioned before the throne of God. Their continual worship conveys a holiness without end. As the Word describes, *"And one cried unto another, and said, Holy, holy, holy, is the Lord of hosts: the whole earth is full of his glory"* (Isaiah 6:3).

MAJESTIC MOTIFS

In order to understand the mystery of these myriads called *serahpim,* let's examine the "motifs" in Scripture.

———— ∼ ————

A __motif__ is a term used by Swedish theologians to describe recurring elements which have symbolic significance.

71

Isaiah 6:1-9 and Revelation 4 pull back the curtain and allow us to see how the seraphim mirror the majesty of God.

THE FIRST MOTIF OF HIS MAJESTY:
IMMORTALITY

The Almighty is without beginning and without end. He alone *"...hath immortality, dwelling in the light which no man can approach"* (1 Timothy 6:16).

In heaven, these six-winged creatures praise Him unceasingly, crying, *"Holy, holy, holy, Lord God Almighty, which was, and is, and is to come"* (Revelation 4:8).

THE SECOND MOTIF OF HIS MAJESTY:
DIVINITY AND INFINITY

The reason the seraphim worship day and night is because they are unable to conceive or perceive the totality of His being.

The Bible says they have, *"...eyes before and*

behind" (Revelation 4:6), and can see the greatness of His past and can point to the praise awaiting them in the future, yet they have never seen God.

———————— 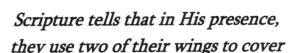 ————————

Scripture tells that in His presence, they use two of their wings to cover their faces (Isaiah 6:2).

THE THIRD MOTIF OF HIS MAJESTY:
SELF-EXISTENCE

One of the divine attributes of God as revealed in the "song of the seraphim" (Isaiah 6:3) is His Self-Existence.

Before time, He was! Scripture declares, *"In the beginning was the Word, and the Word was with God, and the Word was God"* (John 1:1).

The Greek verb "was" is in the imperfect tense, which indicates continuous action in the past. Therefore, as the Self-Existent One, there is never a time the Word *was not.*

This is the God the seraphim continually praise.

THE FOURTH MOTIF OF HIS MAJESTY:
OMNISCIENCE

No created beings are all-knowing, yet the seraphim illustrate and communicate God's omniscient power. Not only do they have eyes *"before and behind"* (Revelation 4:6), *"...they were full of eyes within"* (v.8).

This leaves much to the imagination, yet it is a motif which represents an all-seeing, all-knowing God.

The psalmist says, *"Lord, thou hast searched me, and known me. Thou knowest my downsitting and mine uprising, thou understandest my thought afar off...Such knowledge is too wonderful for me, it is high and I cannot attain it"* (Psalm 139:1-2,6).

THE BURNING, BLAZING LOVE FROM ABOVE

The Hebrew word *seraph* means "to burn"—indicating theses angels are on fire with the love of God.

Remember, the Almighty spoke to Moses through a burning bush, demonstrated Himself to Elijah on Mount Carmel as a fire and sent His Holy Spirit to the believers in the Upper Room as *"...cloven tongues like as of fire"* (Acts 2:3).

The closer we draw to Him, the more Christlike we become—blazing and burning with the passion of His love.

PREPARATION FOR A REVELATION

To better comprehend the purpose of seraphim we need to explore the context in which they were introduced in Scripture.

In the land of Judah, a young man named Uzziah became king at the age of 16 and reigned in Jerusalem for 52 years. At the beginning of his leadership he proved to be a gifted monarch and his accomplishments on the field of battle were legendary.

For example, Uzziah was the first one in Israel to invent a cannon to be used in battle (2 Chronicles 26:15). The people marveled at how he was able to wage war and *"...as long as he sought the Lord, God made him to prosper"* (v.5).

The day arrived, however, when Uzziah became so filled with pride, conceit and arrogance it was his downfall. The Bible says, *"...when he was strong, his heart was lifted up to his destruction"* (v.16).

Because of his ego and self-importance, one day he walked into the temple to burn incense on the altar. This was absolutely prohibited by sacred law since you could not enter the inner court unless you were a priest.

Uzziah was neither a Levite or a priest, yet because of his position as a powerful king, he grabbed a censer to burn the incense and pushed his way in, completely disrespecting the written commands of God.

Scripture records how the king became extremely upset and belligerent when the priests attempted to block his entrance. Then, suddenly, disaster struck: *"...leprosy...rose up in his forehead before the priests in* the house of the Lord, from beside the incense altar" (v.19).

Immediately, the high priest threw the king out of the temple *"...because the Lord had smitten him"* (v.20).

Uzziah remained a leper until the day of his death. To Jews, the throne room of God was on the mercy seat of the Ark of the Covenant and the laws governing who could enter the inner sanctuary and the Holy of Holies were extremely specific.

"HOLY, HOLY, HOLY!"

After the king's demise, we read of a man named Isaiah who had a vision from God. *"In the year that king Uzziah died I saw also the Lord sitting upon a throne, high and lifted up, and his train filled the temple"* (Isaiah 6:1).

Above the throne *"...stood the seraphims: each one had six wings; with twain he covered his face, and with twain he covered his feet, and with twain he did fly. And one cried unto another, and said, Holy, holy, holy, is the Lord of hosts: the whole earth is full of his glory"* (vv.2-3).

Most people I speak with have a difficult time

envisioning a six-winged angel. Because of the rendering of artists we are used to seeing them robed in white adorned with only two wings.

Yet the angel Isaiah saw in his vision was a seraphim—a six-winged creature. Again, two wings were specifically designed to cover their face because the holiness of the Lord is so bright, no man can possibly stand before Him—they had to protect their sight.

THE POWER OF HIS PRESENCE

What can we make of Isaiah's experience? He was not a priest, just a man receiving a call to become a prophet. In the natural he knew he had no business approaching the throne of heaven, yet through a vision, he was allowed to enter.

———— ∼ ————

Who did Isaiah see sitting on the throne? Was it God?

We know from scripture that God is a Spirit and no

one has seen Him. We are also commanded not to make any graven images of His supposed likeness. He told Moses, *"Thou canst not see my face: for there shall no man see me, and live"* (Exodus 33:20).

Instead, God asked Moses to stand in the cleft of the rock while His glory was near, and He said, *"[I] will cover thee with my hand while I pass by"* (v.22).

A MESSIANIC MESSAGE

I believe the One whom Isaiah saw in his vision was Jesus— *"the glory of God"* (2 Corinthians 4:6; Revelation 21:23). It was *"...the brightness of his glory, and the express image of his person"* (Hebrews 1:3).

Isaiah was allowed to enter the true throne room because he was the Messianic prophet. Not only was he going to address Israel concerning the coming Messiah, he now could speak from personal experience.

Uzziah was not permitted by God to enter the throne room, and Isaiah could only see it through a vision, but because of Christ, our new high priest, you and I can *"...come boldly unto the throne of grace, that we may obtain mercy, and find grace to help in time of need"* (Hebrews 4:16).

SINGING OF THE SON

Isaiah was anointed to become the voice who revealed the coming Christ. At the time of his writing, Israel was in turmoil, so how could the earth be "filled with His glory"? (Isaiah 6:3).

This was the song of the seraphim, singing of the day when the Son of God would be born in Bethlehem and *"...the angel of the Lord came upon them, and the glory of the Lord shone round about them"* (Luke 2:9).

Isaiah was overwhelmed with what God entrusted him to glimpse. So much so he cried, *"Woe is me! for I am undone; because I am a man of unclean lips, and I dwell in the midst of a people of unclean lips: for mine eyes have seen the King, the Lord of hosts. Then flew one of the seraphims unto me, having a live coal in his hand, which he had taken with the tongs from off the altar: And he laid it upon my mouth, and said, Lo, this hath touched thy lips; and thine iniquity is taken away, and thy sin purged"* (Isaiah 6:5-7).

PARDONED AND PURGED

This is the first and only time in the old covenant that someone's sins were totally removed. We know the Word declares without the shedding of blood there is no remission of sin (Hebrews 9:22), so how was this possible?

The blood of bulls and goats on the altar of sacrifice could not eradicate iniquity—only cover it temporarily. What took place on the Day of Atonement in Israel could only provide covering of sin until the next year.

Isaiah, however, was permitted to enter the mercy seat. This is where the blood was offered, which was guaranteed from *"...the Lamb slain from the foundation of the world"* (Revelation13:8).

It was because he was granted permission to enter into the Holy of Holies in heaven itself that his sins were purged.

WINGS OF WORSHIP

There is a parallel between the throne room experience described in John's revelation and the sanctuary of the seraphim.

This passage, which we briefly referred to earlier, tells how *"...round about the throne, were four beasts [angels] full of eyes before and behind. And the first beast was like a lion, and the second beast like a calf, and the third beast had a face as a man, and the fourth beast was like a flying eagle. And the four beasts had each of them six wings about him; and they were full of eyes within: and they rest not day and night, saying, Holy, holy, holy, Lord God Almighty, which was, and is, and is to come"* (Revelation 4:7-8).

Once more—just as depicted by Isaiah—the six-winged seraphim were worshiping with the words: "Holy, holy, holy, Lord God Almighty."

The angels do not rest or grow weary because theirs is a song which never ends.

Even when the angels are executing judgment, they

cry out *"...with a loud voice, Worthy is the Lamb that was slain to receive power, and riches, and wisdom, and strength, and honour, and glory, and blessing"* (Revelation 5:12).

Repeatedly in Revelation we find the angels exalting, because they cannot contain the glory and holiness of God.

I can tell you on the authority of the Word that one day soon you and I will be standing around the same throne with tears streaming down our faces.

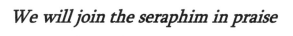

We will join the seraphim in praise and worship to the Lord.

What a glorious day it will be!

Lord Jesus, I ask you to draw me to the place of Your presence and allow me to behold your beauty as the seraphim.

Grant that the closer I am to You, the more I will become a flame of fire—ablaze with the love of God.

*Holy Spirit, join my song with the seraphim
as I sing, Holy, Holy Holy.*

Amen.

CHAPTER FIVE

WHEELS IN THE WIND

The appearance of the wheels and
their work was like unto the colour of a beryl:
and they four had one likeness: and their
appearance and their work was as it were
a wheel in the middle of a wheel.

– EZEKIEL 1:16

The image most people have of an angel is one of a heavenly being with two wings. Since this is the way most artists and sculptors depict them, this picture is etched in our mind.

Even more, we have relegated the wings of angels for the sole purpose of flying. But as we saw in the last chapter, there are certain types of angels who possess *more* than two wings?

Consider the dynamic detail of the cherubim: *"...and their wings were stretched upward; two wings of every one were joined one to another, and two covered their bodies"* (Ezekiel 1:11).

The text teaches that specific species of angels have wings which are *not* used for flying. The context conveys there is a majestic movement manifested by the glory of God in the wings of the cherubim. Their four wings are lifted by the wind. *"And every one had four faces, and every one had four wings"* (v.6).

Scripture also tells us, *"And when the living creatures went, the wheels went by them: and when the living creatures were lifted up from the earth, the wheels were lifted up. Whithersoever the spirit was to go, they went, thither was their spirit to go; and the wheels were lifted up over against them: for the spirit of the living creature was in the wheels"* (vv.19-20).

FROM DESOLATION
TO REVELATION

Ezekiel chapter one contains a miraculous message:

- To all who feel distanced from their dream.
- To all who feel detached from their destiny.
- To all who are in the stronghold of spiritual exile.

What do I mean by "spiritual exile?" It is a condition of captivity which isolates and separates from the design of destiny in your life.

If you are in despair and feel God doesn't care, here is a word of comfort to the captives: "...the heavens were opened, and I saw visions of God" (v.1).

For Ezekiel, in the time of his greatest desolation came the revelation of an open heaven. The prophet priest stood in awe, glimpsing the glory of the celestial city.

Four winged creatures were being carried by the wind—and Ezekiel 10:2-9 tells us these creatures are the cherubim. What he witnessed while in Babylon was supernatural.

FORWARD THROUGH FIRE

Based on the biblical pattern in Ezekiel, there are four prophetic principles which clarify and identify the ways of worship paralleled in the cherubim.

First: There is a corporate connection woven in their wings.

"Their wings were joined one to another; they turned not when they went; they went every one straight forward" (Ezekiel 1:9).

**Everything in heaven is perfected because
it is connected by love.**

Remember, *"...wings of every one were joined one to another"* (v.11).

Second: Sensitivity to the Spirit propels their power.

"And they went every one straight forward:

whither the spirit was to go, they went; and they turned not when they went" (v.12).

This is important: " ***Whithersoever the spirit was to go, they went, thither was their spirit to go...***" (v.20).

The cherubim moved only by the motion of the Spirit. This is a prophetic prefiguring of all who walk in the anointing.

If your willingness is completed, your anointing will not be depleted. This means when we access the anointing it is only because we have totally and unconditionally surrendered to the Spirit of God.

Third: The focus is forward.

Scripture accentuates and punctuates this focus: *"...they went every one straight forward"* (Ezekiel 1:9).

The personal prophetic application is that the cherubim were *always* yielded to the Spirit.

When everything in our lives becomes conformed and consumed by His leading, we will always advance because of the anointing.

Fourth: There is perfected praise from a furnace of fire.

In the words of Ezekiel, *"...out of the midst thereof as the colour of amber, out of the midst of the fire. Also out of the midst thereof came the likeness of four living creatures"* (vv.4-5).

The cherubim arose out of the fire and prophetically paralleled perfect praise!

———— ～ ————

Fire is a purifying power—and through fire that purges, worship emerges.

WHEELS WITHIN WHEELS

Can you visualize angels with both wings and wheels? This is what Ezekiel beheld as he watched wheels turning and burning by the power of the Spirit.

The prophet writes: *"Now as I beheld the living creatures, behold one wheel upon the earth...[and] their appearance and their work was as it were a wheel in the middle of a wheel....and when the living creatures were lifted up from the earth, the wheels were lifted up. Whithersoever the spirit was to go, they went, thither was their spirit to go; and the wheels were lifted up over against them: for the spirit of the living creature was in the wheels"* (vv:15-16,19-20).

God is not, like us, confined or limited in time, space or how He chooses to operate.

These wheels propel the power of God from heaven to earth. *"And when the cherubims went, the wheels went by them: and when the cherubims lifted up their wings to mount up from the earth, the same wheels also turned not from beside them"* (Ezekiel 10:16).

The prophet Daniel describes in deeper detail this work of wonder: *"I beheld till the thrones were cast down, and the Ancient of days did sit, whose garment was white as snow, and the hair of his head like the pure wool: his throne was like the fiery flame, and his wheels as burning fire"* (Daniel 7:9).

Cherubim came down from heaven (Ezekiel 1 and 10) as the chariot of God to lift the glory off the Holy City and the temple before the invasion of the Babylonians. *"Then the glory of the Lord departed from off the threshold of the house, and stood over the cherubims. And the cherubims lifted up their wings, and mounted up from the earth in my sight: when they went out, the wheels also were beside them, and every one stood at the door of the east gate of the Lord's house; and the glory of the God of Israel was over them above"* (Ezekiel 18-19).

The text teaches that the chariot of God, in the form of the cherubim, descended to lift the glory off the temple in *stages.* The Babylonians could not invade or raid God's house or the Holy City as long as the glory remained on it.

In personal prophetic terms, we need the glory in our lives as a wall of protection over our children, homes and careers. It is written: *"For I, saith the Lord, will be unto her a wall of fire round about, and will be the glory in the midst of her"* (Zecariah 2:5).

When the glory descends, our exile ends.

UTTERING BY FLUTTERING

Continuing in the context of Ezekiel 1, the Master

of Creation created wings of the cherubim to be in position for the purpose of power. When their wings wave in the wind, there is a shift into sounds by the Spirit of God.

The prophet proclaims a divine utterance was heard in heaven by the synchronized sounds of fluttering wings. *"And when they went, I heard the noise of their wings, like the noise of great waters, as the voice of the Almighty, the voice of speech, as the noise of an host: when they stood, they let down their wings"* (Ezekiel 1:24).

This means when wings fluttered, God's voice uttered! The rustlings released a resounding of His Word. *"And there was a voice from the firmament that was over their heads, when they stood, and had let down their wings"* (v.25).

In everything, wings wield worship to God.

Adoration produced a proclamation of His Word in the heavens.

As the wings flapped, earth became enrapt in His presence. *"And the sound of the cherubims' wings was heard even to the outer court, as the voice of the Almighty God when he speaketh"* (Ezekiel 10:5).

COVERING AND HOVERING OVER THE GLORY OF GOD

The cherubim are the selected, elected specie of angels which enthrone the glory of God.

The very first place cherubim appear is in the Garden of Eden. When Adam lost his ministry to guard the glory, his position was replaced by these heavenly angels. *"And the Lord God* [Adonai Eloheim] *took the man, and put him into the garden of Eden to dress it and to keep it"* (Genesis 2:15).

Let's investigate the text further. In Hebrew, the verb "to dress" is the word *abad*—a term which denotes labor and service. It is a verb that concisely and precisely indicates servitude.

Adam's mission and mantle was a priestly one. He is given the position for the purpose of priesthood in the garden.

The text emphasizes "to dress it and to keep it." And the verb "to keep" in Hebrew is the word *shamar*—often used in the context of a watchman. It literally means "to guard," and denotes attending something.

Remember, when Adam lost his ministry in the garden through the fall, it was replaced by the cherubim. As scripture records, *"So he drove out the man; and he placed at the east of the garden of Eden Cherubims, and a flaming sword which turned every way, to keep the way of the tree of life"* (Genesis 3:24).

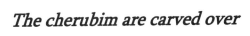

The cherubim are carved over the Ark of the Covenant.

Their wings cover the ark as a symbolic similitude of hovering and covering. *"And the cherubims shall stretch forth their wings on high, covering the mercy seat with their wings..."* (Exodus 25:20).

These four-winged creatures stretch two wings

upward and two wings over the ark, prophetically paralleling lifting praise to the highest pinnacle of power.

Because of the blood of Jesus, what Adam forfeited is now fulfilled. Beloved, we have been purchased for the purpose of priesthood. *"Unto him that loved us, and washed us from our sins in his own blood, and hath made us kings and priests unto God and his Father"* (Revelation 1:5-6).

———— ∾ ————

What Adam lost has been paid by the cost of Calvary.

MESSIANIC TRACES IN THE FACES OF THE CHERUBIM

All angels from every rank and species are a reflection of the perfection of the Son of God. Each of the myriads and multitudes in their being proclaim and acclaim His endless glory. He is the Creator of all angels: *"For by him were all things created, that are in*

heaven, and that are in earth..." (Colossians 1:16).
"And "...he saith...let all the angels of God worship him" (Hebrews 1:6).

Continuing in the context of Ezekiel 1, there is a Calvary connection in the focus of the cherubim. As we have seen, *"Their wings were joined one to another; they turned not when they went; they went every one straight forward"* (Ezekiel 1:9). But pay close attention to this: ***"As for the likeness of their faces, they four had the face of a man, and the face of a lion, on the right side: and they four had the face of an ox on the left side; they four also had the face of an eagle"*** (v.10).

This narrative reveals the nature of divine attributes. In their faces, the text traces the Messiah of Israel, Jesus Christ.

Everything in heaven points to the praise of the Son of God:

- *The face of a man* declares and lauds the life of Jesus, who became Man for our sake (John 1:14).

- *The face of a lion* declares the destiny of the Messiah, the Lion of Judah (Genesis 49:9; Revelation 5:6).
- *The face of an ox* symbolizes supreme sacrifice. The ox is the most costly of all sacrifices in Israel (Revelation 1:3-9).
- The face of an eagle denotes dominion in the heavens, above all principalities and powers (Colossians 2:15).

"SUDDENLY—A SOUND"

One of the reasons God has given His angels charge over us is so our environment can truly become this desired place of praise, worship and thanksgiving.

Note closely what the scripture says concerning the wings of angels. *"Then the spirit took me up, and I heard behind me a voice of a great rushing, saying, Blessed be the glory of the Lord from his place. I heard also the noise of the wings of the living creatures that touched one another, and the noise of the wheels over against them, and a noise of a great rushing"* (Ezekiel 3:12-13).

Notice the words, "Blessed be the glory of the Lord from His place." This speaks of the angels moving their wings, causing praises to erupt.

It is also significant that when the wings of the angels moved, the noise of "a great rushing" was heard.

If this sounds familiar, it is because of what took place on the day of Pentecost. As the 120 were gathered in the Upper Room waiting for the promise of the Father, *"...suddenly there came a sound from heaven as of a rushing mighty wind, and it filled all the house where they were sitting"* (Acts 2:2).

Ezekiel had a preview of this great move of the Spirit.

I pray your atmosphere will become so charged with the glory of God that you worship and praise Him continually.

SURRENDERED TO THE SPIRIT

When angels' wings are in motion, it is as if they

are completely yielded to the activity of the Almighty. When He moves, they move in unison—quickened by the Holy Spirit.

———— ∽ ————

As believers, we can look at these heavenly beings as examples to emulate.

Angelic creatures are so sensitive to the Spirit, they don't change positions without His specific guidance and approval.

If we rush ahead of the Spirit and operate in the flesh, we will block the flow of anointing. This is why it is vital for us to become so sensitive and responsive to God that we only step forward when He does—and when He stops, so do we.

By mirroring what the Holy Spirit is doing at all times, the anointing will continually flow through us to others.

A BLUEPRINT FOR BLESSING

The wings of the cherubim, hovering over the

Ark of the Covenant—more specifically, over the mercy seat—reveal to us the Son of God in His Messianic mission.

God told Moses to make a visible structure to show the children of Israel what spiritual, heavenly things look like. The Lord also gave precise instructions regarding how to build the tabernacle and all the furnishings. There was a detailed blueprint for Moses to follow.

Through the wings of the cherubim, Moses had a "type" of encounter with the blood of Jesus and he was able to hear the voice of God between their wings (Exodus 25:22).

As we have already seen, you and I can also hear the Lord speak through the wings of angels. When the Spirit moves, it delivers the voice of God. How marvelous!

Always remember, what we read in the Old Testament foreshadows salvation and the redemptive work of the Messiah. It points to the triumphant coming to earth of the Son of God.

Praise the Lord!

Meeting at the Mercy Seat

At God's command, Moses finished the construction of the tabernacle with the Ark of the Covenant on which the mercy seat sits. This was called the Throne of God.

Here are the Lord's next instructions: *"And the cherubims shall stretch forth their wings on high, covering the mercy seat with their wings, and their faces shall look one to another; toward the mercy seat shall the faces of the cherubims be"* (Exodus 25:20).

There was a cherub situated on each side of the Ark, facing each other—and their wings covered the mercy seat.

The passage continues, *"And thou shalt put the mercy seat above upon the ark; and in the ark thou shalt put the testimony that I shall give thee. And there I will meet with thee, and I will commune with thee from above the mercy seat, from between the two cherubims which are upon the ark of the testimony, of all things which I will give thee in commandment unto the children of Israel"* (vv.21-22).

BOUGHT WITH HIS BLOOD

You may ask, "What does all this have to do with my life?"

The Messianic revelation—which affects us today —is part of God's law. *"And he shall take of the blood of the bullock, and sprinkle it with his finger upon the mercy seat eastward; and before the mercy seat shall he sprinkle of the blood with his finger seven times"* (Leviticus 16:14).

On the day of Atonement, Aaron was to take the blood and disperse it on the mercy seat between the wings of the cherubim.

This act foreshadows for you and me that it is through the blood of Christ we are redeemed.

Remember, like the wings of angels, the blood also speaks—and it spoke to Moses. This is why the writer of Hebrews says, *"the blood...speaketh"* (Hebrews 12:24).

It was the blood foretelling the sacrifice of Christ which allowed Moses to hear from God between the wings of the angels atop the Ark of the Covenant.

If there had not been a guarantee that the Lord Jesus would someday place His blood on the mercy seat of heaven, Moses would have never heard the voice of God. It was because of Mashiach—the "Anointed One"—and His ministry in the old covenant, that the leader of the children of Israel was able to hear the voice of the Almighty in such an unusual manner.

God sends His ministering angels to deliver messages from the Father directly to us.

ANGELS, AFFLICTION AND THE ALMIGHTY

Perhaps as you read these pages you are anxious or hurting inside—afraid of what tomorrow holds. Or you may be going through trying circumstances. I want to show you how the wings of angels can bring tender mercies to your life today. I believe this will give you a deeper understanding and appreciation of God's love for each of His children.

Scripture tells us, *"In all their affliction he was afflicted, and the angel of his presence saved them: in his love and in his pity he redeemed them; and he bare them, and carried them all the days of old"* (Isaiah 63:9).

This shows the deep emotion which comes from the Father to you and me.

God is so intimate with His sons and daughters that He feels every twinge of their pain. He is afflicted as we are afflicted.

"FEATHERS" AND "WINGS"

I love the words of the psalmist. He writes, *"Surely he shall deliver thee from the snare of the fowler, and from the noisome pestilence. He shall cover thee with his feathers, and under his wings shalt thou trust: his truth shall be thy shield and buckler"* (Psalm 91:3-4).

Does this mean our God has feathers and wings? Not at all!

Again this scripture emphasizes the Lord has specific emissaries which He created before the foundation of the world. More important, He made angels with you in mind. They are in God's Kingdom to take care of you—as His hands extended.

By saying we are covered by His feathers and are under His wings lets us know God formed angels to be one in the Spirit with Him, carrying out the will of the Almighty. It's the Lord's work, yet He uses His angels to fulfill the mission.

Under His covering we are shielded from every adversary.

May this be your prayer today:

Lord Jesus, I fall on my face before You. Let my life be as yielded as the cherubim. Help me lift Your praise to the highest pinnacle of power in my life.

Help me guard the gifts and graces You have freely given me. I want to cover Your majesty with songs and praises, lauding Your Lordship. Help me to become sensitive to the Spirit as the cherubim who move by the Spirit.

Let my praise emerge as You purge my life—just as the cherubim who praise out of the midst of fire. Let me experience the brush of angel's wings on my ears. I desire to hear Your voice in all I do.

Amen.

CHAPTER SIX

THERE'S AN ANGEL ASSIGNED TO YOU!

Be not forgetful to entertain strangers: for thereby
some have entertained angels unawares.
– HEBREWS 13:2

Have you ever experienced the wings of love sent from above by God's secret agents? Perhaps you have and didn't even know it!

Angels appear in the most peculiar places. Sometimes they are sent to the subways in the midst of the hustle and bustle of New York City. Or, an angel can be hidden behind the face of a strange looking man who helps you with the jumper cables for your car.

Sometimes angels are sent to test you before God will bless you—like the time you helped that little man pushing his cart in the rain, feeling his pain. Then, suddenly, a silent, unseen miracle happened. You realized weeks later your unexpected financial blessing came in days after you helped him.

May I share with you how God's tender touch extends from heaven to earth through "angels unawares"?

FROM DETOUR TO DESTINY

It was a stifling hot July evening, about 5:30 P.M. For over an hour I had slowly made my way through bumper-to-bumper traffic on the Santa Monica freeway toward Oxnard in Southern California.

I was twenty-two years old and was headed to a mission outreach of a church I was involved with.

Suddenly, as I was in the far left lane near the Crenshaw exit in South Central Los Angeles, steam started rising from under the hood of my much-used

1970 Hornet. "Oh no," I said to myself, "I have to get this car off the freeway!"

Don't ask me how, but I somehow maneuvered the vehicle through several lanes of traffic and made it to the exit. Directly in front of me was a gas station—a run down place with an auto repair shop. Unfortunately, the business was closed.

Quickly, I shut off the engine and jumped out of the overheated car. To say I looked out of place is an understatement. I was all dressed up in a gorgeous outfit I had purchased at a second-hand clothing store and I felt like a million bucks!

Now I was stranded by my car, worried the oil and water was going to splatter my beautiful dress.

Out of nowhere, an African-American man walked over to me and asked, "Ma'am, do you need some help?"

"Yes, sir," I responded, "I certainly do. I'm on my way to church in Oxnard and I really have to be there on time. I don't know what has happened to my car."

He raised the hood, lifted up his head and said, "Looks like you blew a water pump."

Worried, I exclaimed, "Oh goodness. How much is that going to cost?"

I didn't even have five dollars in my purse."

He said, "You know, ma'am, all of the stores and auto shops are closed, but let me call around for you." He walked over to a phone booth and started dialing.

PAY FOR THE PUMP?

A few minutes later, he returned and smiled, "I located a water pump on the other side of town. I'll go get it for you."

I hesitated, then responded "Sir, I don't have any money to pay for it."

"Don't worry," he said. Then, with a knowing look, he told me something I didn't quite understand at that moment: "You'll pay later," he told me.

In about 30 minutes, he returned with the pump, and had it installed in a jiffy.

As he finished, I asked him, "Can I just get your name and phone number so I can pay you back?"

He replied, "Really, ma'am, you don't have to."

I persisted, "But please, you've been so kind, and have helped me more than you know."

Reluctantly, he wrote down a number—but no name.

I turned around briefly to get into my car. And when I looked back, after only a short moment, he was gone. I marveled at how quickly the man had disappeared from the parking lot. He appeared to have simply vanished.

MICHELLE? A MINISTER?

That night, I arrived at the church around 8:00 P.M. and rushed into the auditorium to find a seat.

The pastor was making plans for the future of the outreach ministry, but a man named Kelly, whom he had intended to assign as a minister at this particular location, was not present. So the pastor needed another person who would make a commitment to preach there once each month.

In front of a packed church, the pastor announced, "Kelly is not here tonight. Who can we choose to replace him and take this assignment?"

I can't explain how shocked I was when he pointed directly at me and said, "Michelle, you are the one. The Lord is calling you to minister and now is the time. Will you please come forward?"

A SHOCKING SURPRISE

God had appointed a man to do this job, yet since he didn't show up, I was the one chosen.

I ran nervously to the front of the church. The pastor told me, "Michelle, you are going to return and train these workers in the Word of God. Your specialty will be teaching them how to move in sensitivity to the Holy Spirit. You will prepare these workers to help me in my miracle services."

I was still surprised, but thrilled.

Earlier, at the age of sixteen, I felt the call of God

on my life to serve Him in missionary work, yet now I was being appointed to a more defined ministry—to preach!

Shortly after this appointment I conducted my first service—and I've been preaching the precious Gospel ever since. It was my destiny to proclaim how to obtain access to the anointing.

THE ANGEL WHO PAVED THE PATH

The Monday after the "water pump" incident, I told my brother, George, "I need to pay the man who repaired my car."

We dialed the number repeatedly, but there was never a connection.

There is not one doubt in my mind this African-American gentleman was an angel sent of God—preparing the way for my first ministry assignment.

Had I not reached Oxnard that night, the opportunity for the launching of my ministry would not have occurred.

I experienced what the psalmist wrote, *"For he shall give his angels charge over thee, to keep thee in all thy ways"* (Psalm 91:11).

LOST IN EAST L.A.

Looking back, this was not the first time God had provided an angel to watch over my life.

I remember very little concerning my early childhood, yet one memory will be forever seared in my memory.

As a three and four-year old, in the 1950s, I loved to go downtown with my mom and grandmother. We lived in East Los Angeles.

On our weekly excursions, we would stop for a cool drink from the soda fountain at Thrifty's Drug Store, then continue on to Woolworth's and the Learner's dress shop.

One day, when my mother had let go of my hand just for a minute, I decided to take off and explore all the stores by myself.

After a brief few moments of freedom, I realized I was lost and my eyes began to fill with tears.

"Where's my mommy?" I whimpered. I was frightened and couldn't find her anywhere.

Eventually, the flashing lights of police cars were all around me. Then a wonderful woman, who I can only remember as an angel, took me by the hand and led me straight to my distraught mother for the best reunion ever!

A Nigerian Nightmare!

You can rest assured when the Lord is guiding your life, He is always watching, protecting and providing a way where there seems to be no way.

I remember when my husband and I followed God's call to the mission field—first in the Philippines and then in Africa.

In 1980, we spent considerable time in a remote area of southeastern Nigeria. It was a center for witchcraft and animal worship where killing for revenge was a common practice.

When the day arrived for us to return home, we decided to travel back to the States with five other missionaries. Our plan was to find someone who would drive us to the airport at Calabar—about two hours away—where we would catch a plane to Logos, then an international flight back to the U.S.

A CAR TO CALABAR?

There was only one problem. The Nigerian who had been our host decided we should all remain in his village and absolutely refused to help us find transportation.

We pleaded, "Our work here is finished and we must return to our homes."

"No. You are not leaving," he insisted.

After discussing the matter among ourselves, we decided to get up early the next morning and walk with our luggage to the local dead-end, seldom used road. Perhaps, just perhaps, we could find a person who would drive us to Calabar.

It was a scene I will never forget. Seven missionaries with far too much luggage were standing by the side of the road at five o'clock in the morning—in the pouring rain.

Only one car was in sight. It was a small, beat-up Volkswagen that could not have carried half of us, let alone our luggage!

SMILING STRANGERS

Before long, our soaking wet team was becoming tired and impatient. "Don't worry," I kept assuring them, "The Lord is going to take care of us."

God answered prayer!

It wasn't long before a white station wagon drove

up and the two Nigerian men inside asked, "Where are you going?"

"We have to get to the airport at Calabar to catch a plane."

With big smiles on their faces, they said, "Don't worry. Hop in."

"How much?" we wanted to know.

Again, they responded, "Don't worry!"

WHO WERE THEY?

Please understand. If you are a foreigner in Nigeria and stuck for transportation it could cost you literally thousands of dollars.

After tying our luggage on top and squeezing ourselves into the station wagon, we were finally on our way out of the jungle.

I am still amazed at the mystery of this journey. The men hardly spoke a word to us. We didn't know who they were or where they were from. Yet, they smiled and sang Gospel songs and hymns all the way to Calabar.

Even more baffling, they dropped us off at the

airport and quickly drove out of sight—never asking for a dollar or even giving us their address.

To this day, I believe with all my heart
the Lord arranged for these men to meet us
in our hour of need. To me, they were
God's angels on assignment.

ASHLEY'S ANGEL

During my years of ministry, people have shared their personal testimonies of how God's guardians have protected and directed them. I am always thrilled and amazed when I hear their stories.

Let me tell you about Ruth, a grandmother who has been a wonderful friend to our outreach. She is a tall, elegant woman with a vibrant personality and a charming Australian accent—who appears far more youthful than her years.

Ruth loves to go on roller coaster rides with her young granddaughter, Ashley. You know, the ones that go backward, upside down and turn your stomach inside out!

This fun-loving grandmother dearly adores her granddaughter.

Whether she is at work among the rich and famous or comforting a drunk or homeless person, Ruth has a heart of gold, always helping those in need.

A SCREECHING STOP

On a bright, sunny day, late in the afternoon, September 2003, Ruth was getting ready to drive to the grocery store in her SUV. She had no earthly idea of the terror which was to grip her in the next few minutes.

Hopping into her vehicle, Ruth entertained only pleasant thoughts on that late summer afternoon.

As she was driving down a hill near her home, with the sun glaring in her eyes, suddenly blinded, she couldn't see the road ahead.

At that moment, she heard a loud thump against her car and Ruth thought she had hit a dog. Her eyes quickly darted to the side view mirror in time to see a child being hurled through the air. She screeched on the brakes, jumped out of the car and cried out, "Oh, my Lord! It's Ashley, my granddaughter!"

A CHERISHED CHILD

The girl, who is fatherless on this earth, was the apple of her grandmother's eye. For Ashley, Ruth provided security and emotional stability—but most of all love. The two had a special, loving relationship and you'd often see them arm in arm—enjoying each other's company.

Ashley delighted in going to church with her granny, and Ruth had always known God had His hand resting on this little girl who loved to pray.

With her oval face, clear blue eyes, golden blond hair and that certain innocence little girls possess, Ashley looked like an angel herself.

CAUGHT ON A CLOUD

In this moment of tragedy, Ruth frantically rushed to the back of her car, her heart racing. She saw her granddaughter sprawled on the street next to her twisted bike. Ruth was crying hysterically.

Not even thinking how seriously Ashley might be injured, Ruth tenderly lifted the little girl into her car to drive her to the hospital.

Ashley was her only granddaughter and she had taken care of her for at least seventy five percent of her young life. Ruth was so shaken over what had just happened, she thought, "How can I even drive this car?"

She just kept crying out the name of Jesus.

Suddenly, Ashley turned her eyes toward her grandmother and asked, "Granny why are you crying? I am okay."

Stunned, Ruth looked down at her in disbelief and said, "What did you say Ashley?"

Again she replied, "Granny don't cry. I'm okay. An angel caught me—and it felt like I fell on a cloud."

A MIRACLE OF MERCY

Ruth examined her and didn't find even a scratch on her little body. Ashley was smiling, but Ruth was still shaken and in a state of shock.

A woman who witnessed the accident rushed over and asked, "What hospital are you taking her to?"

Without hesitation, Ruth replied, "We're not going to the hospital. Ashley's all right."

"Surely, you're going to have her checked out," the neighbor insisted.

"No," replied Ruth calmly, "The Lord has already taken care of her."

Ruth had no doubt concerning the miracle Jesus, in His mercy, had just performed.

DESCRIBED IN A DREAM

Later that day, Ashley shared with her grandmother a dream she had the night before. "I was

125

walking down the street and another little girl was with me."

"Who was she?" Ruth inquired.

"I really don't know," Ashley replied. "I have never seen her face before." Then she continued, "As I was walking with her, I saw a white car—like yours Granny—coming down the street and the car hit me. I knew it wasn't you because I didn't see the name 'Jesus' like there is on your license plate."

EXAMINING THE EVIDENCE

A few days later, Ruth was going to her church to help decorate for a special event. As she began to open the back door of her SUV, she noticed something unusual on the window. "It looked like a pair of angel wings," she told me.

Ruth had never seen anything like this before and she drew closer to examine the wings which were pure white with fine ridges—like a feather.

She and her friend, Annette, touched them and oil came off on their fingers. Ruth trembled, realizing this was a visible sign an angel was looking after her precious granddaughter.

Below the wings were black marks and dents on the door where Ashley was hurled through the air. "I realized a miracle had taken place and an angel had protected my grandchild from harm," she exclaimed. I personally have viewed the photos Ruth took and you can see the perfect child-size angel wings and the clear feather-like markings.

The protection of God's Guardians will be forever held in the minds of Ruth and her granddaughter—her Heavenly Father's little girl.

Lord Jesus, thank You for sending angels all around me. I claim Psalm 91:11-12 over my children and my household. Because of the blood of Your cross, I receive the love from the Father as a treasure in His sight.

Thank you for assigning angels over everything that concerns me.

Amen.

CHAPTER SEVEN

THE GRIP OF GETHSEMENE

And let all the angels of God worship him.

– HEBREW 1:6

Perhaps at this very moment you are passing through an agonizing, painful place in life. You may feel a loss—or are carrying the weight of a heavy cross.

Let me assure you that God has promised to take you from your grief to the great destiny He has planned. Yes, He has assigned His angels to carry you through the severity of the storm to a place of safety and rest.

When you don't know how you can continue to face the fight for your future, He sends His heavenly beings to assist you.

THE PREFACE TO HIS PASSION

You see, the Son of God endured every trial, temptation and trouble you will ever experience—and more.

The preface to His passion began at the Garden of Gethsemane, located at the foot of the Mount of Olives in Jerusalem. Scripture teaches that in this sacred place, the Father began to "press" His Son into *passion*—which means the "suffering" Christ endured.

The name Gethsemane is derived from the Hebrew word for "olive press."

To understand His indescribable agony we must compare Gethsemane to Leviticus 16, where the text teaches how a scapegoat was chosen on the day of atonement. *"And Aaron shall lay both his hands upon the head of the live goat, and confess over him all the iniquities of the children of Israel, and all their transgressions in all their sins, putting them upon the head of the goat..."* (Leviticus 16:21).

Jesus Christ, foreshadowed in this Scripture, is our atonement.

In every Old Testament sacrifice offered to God, the priest had to *press* or *lean* on the animal. This represented the strength of sin being transfered to the substitute on the altar.

THE SAVIOR'S SORROW

In the Garden of Gethsemane, the Father in heaven laid His hand upon the head of His only Son, as Jesus, our scapegoat, began the experience of taking the unbearable burden of sin in our stead.

Centuries before, God inspired the prophet Isaiah to write, *"All we like sheep have gone astray; we have turned every one to his own way; and the Lord hath laid on him the iniquity of us all"* (Isaiah 53:6).

In this preface to His passion,
unspeakable sorrow began to swallow
up the soul of the Savior.

He cried to His disciples, *"My soul is exceeding sorrowful, even unto death"* (Matthew 26:38).

His sadness and grief was so excruciating He could have collapsed from the agonizing burden of it all before ever reaching Calvary. How was it possible for the Savior to carry His cross after being weighed down with the sin of the world on His shoulders? How could He complete His destiny to die on Calvary when death began to grip Him in Gethsemane? Scripture describes His pain. *"And he went a little farther, and fell on his face, and prayed, saying, O my Father, if it be possible, let this cup pass from me..."* (Matthew 26:39).

The anguish was so immense, as He prayed, *"...his sweat was as it were great drops of blood falling down to the ground"* (Luke 22:44).

CONSENTING TO THE CROSS

I believe the Father not only laid upon Him the heaviness of our sin, but also began to reveal the realities of Calvary to His Son.

Jesus began to understand and experience the

Father's plan for man's redemption. This revelation was necessary because every step He trod toward Golgotha was taken with consent by Christ.

As the result of His conscious agreement, an angel was dispatched from heaven to fortify Jesus. Scripture records, *"And there appeared an angel unto him from heaven, strengthening him"* (Luke 22:43).

Beloved, because of Calvary's covenant, this same power and provision has been afforded you.

Angels have been assigned to give you strength for whatever trial you may be facing.

In the natural, you may feel like giving up because of the circumstances which are crushing in from every side—detouring the path to your destiny. Perhaps you have even cried to yourself, saying, "I don't have the stamina to survive or to revive my dream."

Look again at the example of Jesus. Once you consent to carry your "small" cross—and it really is just that compared with what Christ carried—help from heaven is on the way. God will send His angels to lift your spirits, lighten the load and renew your hope.

ANGELS ASCENDING AND DESCENDING

Jesus lived His life under a continuous "open heaven"—meaning the atmosphere around Him was filled with angels. They were constantly ascending and descending from heaven to earth to assist God's Son.

We read how the windows of heaven parted over Him just before He began His public ministry. At the river Jordan, He offered Himself in total consecration and separation unto God, His Father. The Bible tells us, *"Now when all the people were baptized, it came to pass, that Jesus also being baptized, and praying, the heaven was opened"* (Luke 3:21).

In His earthly form as a Man, He surrendered to the Holy Spirit in every area of His life. Even before Jesus performed His first miracle at the wedding in Cana, He said to Nathanael, *"Verily, verily, I say unto you, Hereafter ye shall see heaven open, and the angels of God ascending and descending upon the*

Son of man" (John 1:51).

AGREEMENT WITH THE ALMIGHTY

As God's Son, Jesus understood His divine mission on earth, yet was humble as a Man. He was self-existence, without beginning or end. *"And the Word was made flesh, and dwelt among us, (and we beheld his glory, the glory as of the only begotten of the Father,) full of grace and truth"* (John1:14).

While walking the dusty roads, Christ recognized His place—and His dependance on divine strength from above. The writer of Hebrews tells us, *"...we see Jesus, who was made a little lower than the angels for the suffering of death, crowned with glory and honour; that he by the grace of God should taste death for every man"* (Hebrews 2:9).

This gives us a glimpse of how Jesus, in full agreement with the Almighty, surrendered Himself completely in all things to the Holy Spirit during His earthly mission. As a result, from the Scriptures we have just read, we see how angels were around Him continuously.

Friend, you can make a destiny decision today. Like Jesus, you can live under an open heaven.

As you yield your life completely to His leading and the promptings of the Spirit, angels will descend directly to you.

A REFLECTION OF GOD'S PERFECTION

Prayer was a priority in the life of Christ. This is demonstrated and authenticated by His daily sacrifice of surrender.

Every day, Jesus sought out a secret place to commune and fellowship with His Father.

We read, *"And in the morning, rising up a great while before day, he went out, and departed into a solitary place, and there prayed"* (Mark 1:35).

As a result, God sent His angels to guard and protect His Son—and also to ignite the atmosphere.

For Jesus, talking with His Father was an essential

part of a *love* relationship. This is why He could confidently say to Philip, *"...he that hath seen me hath seen the Father"* (John 14:9).

Through constant and consistent prayer, Jesus was a reflection of the perfection of the love of God. *"And it came to pass in those days, that he went out into a mountain to pray, and continued all night in prayer to God"* (Luke 6:12).

THE TASTE OF TRIUMPH

We mentioned earlier how angels are assigned not only for your welfare, but also for your warfare. This was certainly true in the life of Jesus.

For the Son of God, living under an open heaven meant He was required to confront and conquer demonic strongholds.

After His consecration and separation unto God at His baptism, He was led by the Spirit to be "tested" by the devil. *"And he was there in the wilderness forty days, tempted of Satan; and was with the wild beasts; and the angels ministered unto him"* (Mark 1:13).

The three synoptic Gospels tell us of His 40 days in the wilderness. Each one adds more detail of how Jesus dismantles the grip of the enemy.

Mark's insight reveals how for 40 long days He battled with the wild beasts, then, *"...the angels ministered unto him"* (Mark 1:13).

According to Josephus, the historian, "wild beasts" was a term used for demonic spirits.

Angels were sent to strengthen Jesus for the fight. As a result, He lawfully won in His warfare with Satan. These heavenly beings released the victory He had attained through 40 days of fasting and prayer in the desert. *"Who in the days of his flesh, when he had offered up prayers and supplications with strong crying and tears unto him that was able to save him from death, and was heard in that he feared. Though he were a Son, yet learned he obedience by the things which he suffered"* (Hebrews 5:7-8).

Always remember, because of the blood-bought covenant, angels are assigned to you in your struggle against *your* strongholds. As you battle for a breakthrough in prayer and fasting, these angelic beings will give you the taste of triumph in Christ Jesus.

A MANTLE FOR YOUR MISSION

Child of God, when the conflict seems unbearable, know that victory is yours. Angels will literally surround your being—as they did for Jesus. They place a mantle on you for your mission.

Because Christ arose, so can you!

Rejoice in God's power, *"Which he wrought in Christ, when he raised him from the dead, and set him at his own right hand in the heavenly places, far above all principality, and power, and might, and dominion, and every name that is named, not only in this world, but also in that which is to come: and hath put all things under his feet, and gave him to be the head over all things to the church"* (Ephesians 1:20-22).

Will you welcome the angels God has personally assigned to you?

Jesus, I praise You for the victory You won at Calvary's cross. I am risen with You and partake of Your triumph.

Thank You for sending angels to strengthen me in order to fulfill Your will. I ask for a spirit of supplication and prayer so I may live under an open heaven.

I claim that through Your victory, angels assigned to me will ascend and descend over my life until eternity.

Amen.

NOTES

FOR A COMPLETE LIST OF BOOKS,
CD'S AND MINISTRY RESOURCES BY
DR. MICHELLE CORRAL,
CONTACT:

BREATH OF THE SPIRIT MINISTRIES
P. O. BOX 2676
ORANGE, CA 92669

PHONE: 714-695-0668
INTERNET: www.breathofthespirit.org